UNSEEN SCIENCE

What Is Gravity?

Laura L. Sullivan

Cavendish Square
New York

Published in 2016 by Cavendish Square Publishing, LLC
243 5th Avenue, Suite 136, New York, NY 10016

First Edition

Website: cavendishsq.com

This publication represents the opinions and views of the author based on his or her personal experience, knowledge, and research. The information in this book serves as a general guide only. The author and publisher have used their best efforts in preparing this book and disclaim liability rising directly or indirectly from the use and application of this book.

CPSIA Compliance Information: Batch #CW16CSQ

All websites were available and accurate when this book was sent to press.

Library of Congress Cataloging-in-Publication Data

Sullivan, Laura L. (Laura Lee), author.
What is gravity? / Laura L. Sullivan.
pages cm — (Unseen science)
Includes index.
ISBN 978-1-5026-0908-3 (hardcover) ISBN 978-1-5026-0906-9 (paperback) ISBN 978-1-5026-0909-0 (ebook)
1. Gravity—Juvenile literature. I. Title.

QC178.S94 2015
531'.14—dc23

2015017915

Editorial Director: David McNamara
Editor: Andrew Coddington
Copy Editor: Rebecca Rohan
Art Director: Jeffrey Talbot
Designer: Joseph Macri/Amy Greenan
Senior Production Manager: Jennifer Ryder-Talbot
Production Editor: Renni Johnson
Photo Research: J8 Media

The photographs in this book are used by permission and through the courtesy of: Brocreative/Shutterstock.com, cover; Graeme Montgomery/Stone/Getty Images, 5; Tashal/Shutterstock.com, 6; Dorling Kindersley/Getty Images, 7; koya979/Shutterstock.com, 9; BlueRingMedia/Shutterstock.com, 10; Gallileo on the tower of Pisa, McConnell, James Edwin (1903-95)/Private Collection/Look and Learn/Bridgeman Images, 13; Jacek Chabraszewski/Shutterstock.com, 14; Crystal Eye Studio/Shutterstock.com, 15; GIPhotoStock/Science Source, 16; KieferPix/Shutterstock.com, 17; Marius Pirvu/Shutterstock.com, 18; Joggie Botma/Shutterstock.com, 19; Stocktrek/Stockbyte/Getty Images, 21; NASA/age fotostock/Getty Images, 22; NASA, 23, 24; Science Photo Library - Mark Garlick/Brand X Pictures/Getty Images, 25.

Printed in the United States of America

CONTENTS

CHAPTER 1

Understanding Gravity

Gravity is a **force** that we experience every day. It is the reason why things fall down. It gives everything on Earth **weight**. Gravity keeps the Earth orbiting around the sun. It also keeps the moon **orbiting** around the Earth. But what exactly is gravity?

Gravity is the force that attracts, or pulls, all objects toward each other. Gravity acts on everything that has **mass**. All objects, from planets to people, exert gravitational forces on other objects near to them. Larger objects have more gravity. The Earth pulls us down with gravity, keeping us, and everything else on Earth, even air, from flying into space. You also have a gravitational pull on Earth. But you are so tiny compared to the Earth that you never feel it.

Gravity is the force that pulls objects down toward the center of the Earth. In general, it is the force of attraction between any two objects with mass.

The Big Bang and Gravity

Gravity has been around since the beginning of the **universe**. Most scientists think that about fourteen billion years ago, everything that would later become the universe was in a tiny, hot, tightly packed bubble. When that bubble popped in what is known as the **Big Bang**, all matter exploded and expanded, creating our universe.

Time Begins
(Big Bang)

BIG BANG THEORY PHASES

Present Day

When our universe was created in the Big Bang, gravity was the force that attracted individual particles together to eventually form planets and other objects. Gravity is what makes planets round, by pulling matter evenly toward a planet's center.

What Is Gravity?

Isaac Newton was the first scientist to come up with an accurate theory of gravity. He also came up with laws of motion, and other theories to explain how forces worked.

It was gravity that pulled the **atoms** together, forming stars, planets, and moons.

Isaac Newton

Ancient people knew, of course, that when they dropped something it fell. But gravity wasn't defined as a force until an English scientist named Isaac Newton (1642–1727) wrote about it. According to some stories, Newton was sleeping under a tree when an apple fell on his head. This made him wonder why it fell, and he developed his **theory** of gravity.

Theories About Gravity

Now, hundreds of years later, no one understands exactly how gravity works. There are several theories. Some scientists think that all objects exchange particles called **gravitons**. The gravitons bounce between the objects like a game of catch. When they are close, they can "catch" each other's gravitons, and the pull is stronger. When they are farther away, they "drop" more gravitons, and the gravitational pull is weaker.

Other scientists think that an object with mass can actually bend space, causing gravity. Gravity might work with a combination of those two theories.

Gravity and Earth's Orbit

Even if we don't understand all the details of gravity, we can see it in action. Gravity keeps planets in orbit. Objects such as planets tend to move in a straight line unless another force acts on them. Our sun pulls Earth out of the straight line it wants to travel in. But it can't pull the Earth down into the sun because the Earth keeps trying to move straight, too. When both forces act on the Earth, the result is an orbit around the sun.

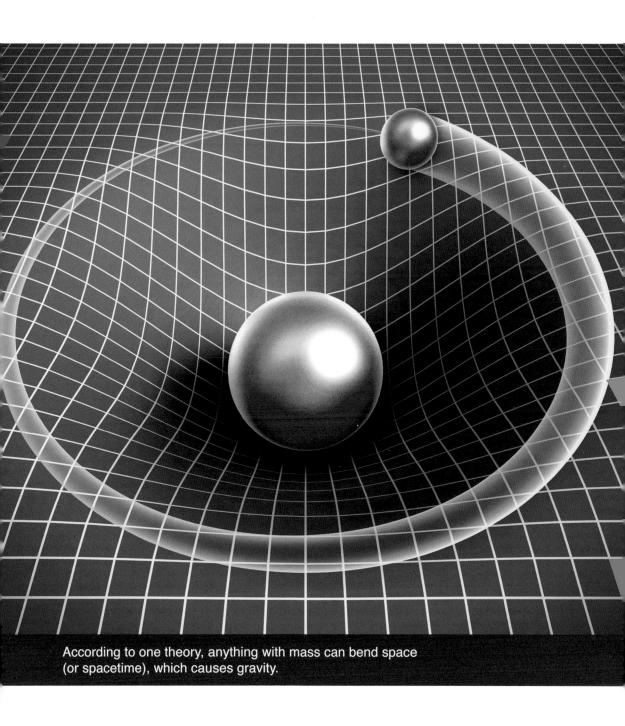

According to one theory, anything with mass can bend space (or spacetime), which causes gravity.

Tidal Changes Caused by Moon's Gravity

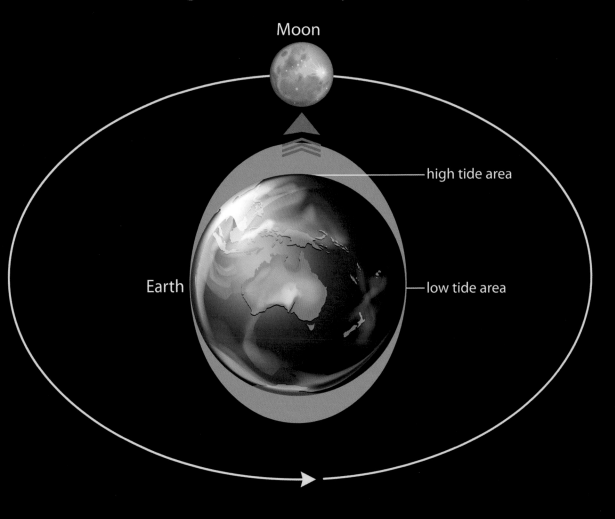

The moon's gravitational pull on Earth's oceans causes the changing tides.
Earth's gravity is pulling on the moon at the same time, keeping it in orbit.

Earth's Oceans and Air

Gravity also causes **tides**. When the moon passes over the earth, it pulls at it. When it pulls on the water, it lifts the water up in a swell. As the moon moves around the Earth, that swell makes high tides.

Gravity even keeps our **atmosphere** in place. If we didn't have an atmosphere, the oxygen we need to breathe would fly out into space. Gravity is one of the things that make life possible.

This Chapter Has Shown

Gravity is the force that pulls objects with mass toward each other. Though scientists don't completely understand how gravity works, they understand its effects. It made stars and planets form after the Big Bang. Gravity also keeps Earth in orbit around the sun. The moon's gravity causes tides.

CHAPTER 2

Gravity in Action

You can see gravity in action with this experiment.

Objective

The Italian scientist Galileo Galilei (1564–1642) performed a famous experiment. He climbed to the top of the Leaning Tower of Pisa, then he dropped balls with different masses over the edge. Galileo thought that everything would fall at the same rate, no matter how big it was. In this project, you will replicate Galileo's experiment in your home or classroom.

Materials

For the basic version of this experiment, you need several objects of different masses that can be safely dropped. You might use:

Galileo performed a famous experiment where he dropped balls of different sizes from the Leaning Tower of Pisa.

- Balls with different masses
- A scarf or a tissue
- A feather

To take this experiment further, you might also need:

- A measuring tape
- A stopwatch
- A ladder, slide, tree, or other hgith place (check with your parents or teacher before using an elevation location)

Procedure

1. Find two objects that you can safely drop. One item should be larger than the other. Two balls with different masses are a good choice. You could also use a sneaker and an apple. Check with a parent or teacher first to make sure you conduct your experiment safely.

2. Hold the items as high as you can, then drop them at exactly the same time. Have a friend watch them land. Note your results.

3. You can make the experiment more scientific by measuring the height from which the objects are dropped. You can also try to time how long it takes them to hit the ground. (It will be difficult to get an exact measurement, though.)

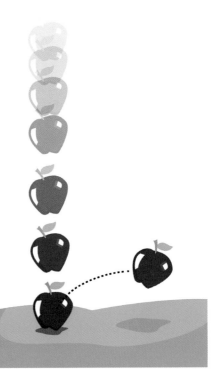

You can repeat your experiment to see if the results stay the same.

Objects on Earth fall at a predictable rate of acceleration, unless another force acts on them.

4. Try a variety of objects and see if your results are the same.

5. With an adult's permission and supervision, try dropping items from someplace higher. You might try the top of playground equipment, or a second-story window.

Questions

- Did the mass of the objects make any difference in how fast they fell?

- Did some objects fall differently than others? Why?

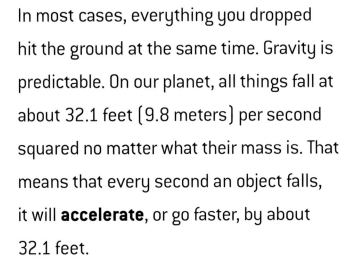
You can show that acceleration due to gravity is a constant by dropping two objects with different weights.

Conclusion

In most cases, everything you dropped hit the ground at the same time. Gravity is predictable. On our planet, all things fall at about 32.1 feet (9.8 meters) per second squared no matter what their mass is. That means that every second an object falls, it will **accelerate**, or go faster, by about 32.1 feet.

If you drop something from a resting position, or zero feet per second, by the end of the first second it will be falling at a **speed** of 32.1 feet (9.8 m) per second. By the next second, it will be traveling at 64.2 feet (19.6 m) per second. At the end of the third second, it will be falling at 96.2 feet (29.3 m) per second. The longer it falls, the faster it will get, up to a point.

When certain light objects like feathers fall, they meet enough air resistance to slow them down. The force of the air pushes up against gravity.

Did you try dropping anything light, like a tissue or a feather? If so, your results might be surprising. Acceleration due to gravity is constant unless some other force acts on the object. If you drop certain things, air can get in the way and slow them down. Air can work against gravity in a force called **air resistance**. That is why a

When a skydiver's parachute opens, the parachute creates more air resistance, slowing the skydiver's fall.

skydiver wearing a parachute falls slowly enough not to get hurt when he lands.

If an object falls far enough, though, it will eventually stop getting faster. It will reach **terminal velocity**. Then, the downward pull of gravity is equaled by the upward push of air resistance. The falling object will stay at the same speed for the rest of the time it falls.

A skydiver in free fall may eventually reach terminal velocity, where the upward push of the air is equal to the downward pull of gravity.

CHAPTER 3

Gravity in Space Science

One of the reasons to study gravity is so we can defy it. When humans figured out how to leave Earth and launch rockets into space, they were escaping gravity's pull. Gravity was still working—it always does—but scientists learned how to make a push that was stronger than gravity's pull.

Escaping Gravity's Pull

Scientists use powerful rockets to blast objects into space. **Satellites** launched into orbit are used to observe locations on

The International Space Station is in orbit around the Earth. It was launched in separate sections and assembled in space.

the Earth, to monitor weather, or to relay communications. The International Space Station also orbits Earth. There, **astronauts** can live and work for long periods, conducting scientific experiments.

A spacecraft needs to travel about 25,000 miles (40,000 kilometers) per hour to escape the earth's gravitational pull and enter space. That's about 7 miles (11 km) per second. If it does not travel fast enough, gravity will pull the spacecraft back to Earth.

A rocket needs a lot of fuel to break free of Earth's gravity and launch into space.

Moving that fast takes a lot of **fuel**. The more the space vehicle weighs, the more fuel it needs to fight Earth's gravity. But fuel also weighs a lot. Scientists must find the right balance between the size of the spacecraft, the weight of its fuel, and the speed needed for a successful launch.

Gravity on Other Planets

Humans have broken free of Earth's gravity to explore the moon. Right now, there are plans to send humans to Mars someday. Though the laws of gravity apply to the entire universe, the effects of gravity are different on different objects in space.

The pull of gravity on the moon, for example, is only about 17 percent of that of Earth. An object dropped on the moon would fall at 5.2 feet (1.6 m) per second squared, compared to 32.1 feet (9.8 m) per second squared on Earth. Low gravity doesn't necessarily

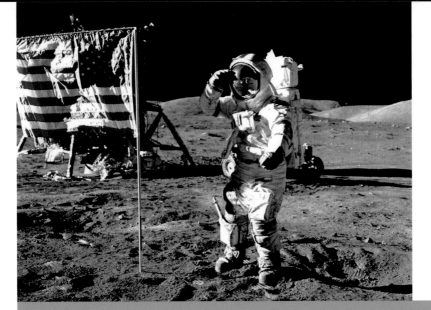

The pull of gravity is weaker on the moon, so astronauts there move very differently than they do on Earth. Sometimes in low gravity, people become confused and disoriented.

turn astronauts into acrobats, though. In lower gravity, it is often hard to know which way is up. People experiencing low gravity can be clumsy.

Mars has about 38 percent of the Earth's gravity. Since that is a little closer to Earth's gravity, an explorer on Mars would probably have an easier time moving there than on the moon.

Risks of Low Gravity

Still, low-gravity environments present problems. Our bodies evolved in Earth's gravity. Our muscles and bones are adapted to a certain amount of gravity. In low gravity, though, our muscles can get weak. Bones even become brittle. Astronauts lose some muscle mass when they go

Astronauts in orbit still experience gravity, but have a sensation of weightlessness because they are essentially in free fall while in orbit. Gravity pulls them down, while their orbital path pulls them sideways, so they feel weightless.

into space. Even though they do special exercises, they are weak when they come back to Earth. The effects would be even worse on a mission to Mars, which would take several years.

Black Holes

Bigger planets such as Jupiter have an even stronger gravitational pull than Earth. But the gravity champion of the universe is a **black hole**. These are regions of space where gravity is so strong it pulls everything around it inside. A black hole can even pull light into it. Nothing can escape the gravitational pull of a black hole.

A black hole exerts so much gravitational pull that all nearby matter is sucked into it. Black holes haven't been directly observed, but their existence is studied by their effect on the rest of space.

This Chapter Has Shown

Rockets defy Earth's gravitational pull by pushing with even more force. Every planet has gravity, but the gravitational pull is weaker on some planets because they are smaller. It is greater on others, because they are massive. Our bodies are used to Earth's gravity and don't always work well in places iwth more or less of it. Black holes have an amazing gravitational pull, sucking in all nearby matter.

GLOSSARY

accelerate To begin to move at a quicker speed.

air resistance The force that air exerts on a moving or falling object.

astronaut A crew member on a craft that is launched into space.

atmosphere The gases that surround the Earth, another planet, or a moon.

atom The smallest particle of an element, which cannot be divided.

Big Bang The theory about the origin of the universe in which all matter was in one dense location, then rapidly expanded.

black hole An area in space with such a strong gravitational field that nothing can escape it, not even light.

force Something that causes a change in motion of an object, such as gravity or air resistance.

fuel A substance that provides energy, power, or heat.

What Is Gravity?

gravitons A hypothesized particle that could be responsible for gravity.

gravity The attraction between all objects with mass; on Earth, the force that causes things to fall toward the center of the Earth.

mass A measurement of how much matter is in objects; weight can change depending on gravity, but mass does not change.

orbit The curved path of one body as it moves around another body in space, such as the movement of the Earth around the sun, or the moon around the Earth.

satellite An object such as a moon, or an artificial object, that orbits around a planet.

speed The rate at which an object moves.

terminal velocity The final speed of a falling object when the upward push of air resistance is equal to the downward push of gravity.

GLOSSARY

theory An explanation for an occurrence that is based on observation or experiments.

tide The falling and rising of sea level that corresponds to the position of the moon.

universe All existing space and matter; the cosmos.

weight A measurement of the force of gravity exerted on an object with mass.

Books

Blobaum, Cindy. *Explore Gravity!: With 25 Great Projects.* White River Junction, VT: Nomad Press, 2013.

Claybourne, Anna. *Gut-Wrenching Gravity and Other Fatal Forces*. New York: Crabtree Publishing Company, 2013.

Jennings, Ken. *Outer Space*. New York: Little Simon, 2014.

Websites

The European Space Agency (ESA)

www.esa.int/ESA

This website has information about space programs and discoveries from Europe's "gateway to space." It has a kids' page that answers many questions.

FIND OUT MORE

The National Aeronautics and Space Administration (NASA)

www.nasa.gov

The NASA site has information about the US space program, the International Space Station, and more, including a page for students.

Physics4Kids

www.physics4kids.com

This site covers many aspects of physics in an easy-to-understand way.

INDEX

Page numbers in **boldface** are illustrations. Entries in **boldface** are glossary terms.

Laura L. Sullivan is the author of more than thirty fiction and nonfiction books for children, including the fantasies *Under the Green Hill* and *Guardian of the Green Hill*. She has written many books for Cavendish Square, including two others in the Unseen Science series: *What Is Heat?* and *What Is Motion?*